Seeds of a Nation

Colorado

Tamra B. Orr

KIDHAVEN PRESS™

THOMSON

GALE

San Diego • Detroit • New York • San Francisco • Cleveland
New Haven, Conn. • Waterville, Maine • London • Munich

For more information, contact
KidHaven Press
27500 Drake Rd.
Farmington Hills, MI 48331-3535
Or you can visit our Internet site at http://www.gale.com

LIBRARY OF CONGRESS CATALOGING-IN-PUBLICATION DATA

Orr, Tamra B.
  Colorado / by Tamra B. Orr.
    p. cm. —— (Seeds of a nation)
Summary: Discusses the early history of Colorado beginning with the Native Americans, through exploration and settlement, to statehood.
Includes bibliographical references and index.
Contents: From Basket Makers to Cliff Dwellers—Discovering the Land—Mountain Men and War—Gold and Statehood
  ISBN 0-7377-1463-8 (alk. paper)
    1. Colorado—Juvenile literature. 2. Colorado—History—Juvenile literature.
I. Title. II. Series.
  F776.3.O77 2003
  978.8—dc21
                               2002009455

Contents

Chapter One

From Basket Makers to Cliff Dwellers

When one looks at the thriving state that Colorado is today, it is hard to believe that it once was a quiet place, with only a few people living there, hunting and foraging for food. With its history of human inhabitants dating back at least twenty-thousand years, Colorado is a state that is rich with history from its very beginnings to the arrival of its statehood.

The Basket Makers

As early as 1500 B.C., a group of people later named the Basket Makers lived in the area now known as Colorado. They were hunters. Their weapons included wooden clubs and hunting sticks. They also used a tool called an **atlatl**, a device that helped them to throw sticks with great force. They lived in caves and under rock overhangs. They wore clothing made from the fur and skin of animals, as well as turkey feather robes and plant fiber sandals. As time went on, these people began to build houses on the **mesas**, or flat-topped mountains. They also dug **kivas**, or underground pits lined with stone, that were used to store the grain they had grown.

Their specialty, however, was making baskets, and that is how they got their name. First, they coiled or braided plant fibers and grasses and then covered them with clay. Next, the baskets were baked until they hardened. All shapes and sizes of baskets were made, often with elaborate designs on them. They were used for all

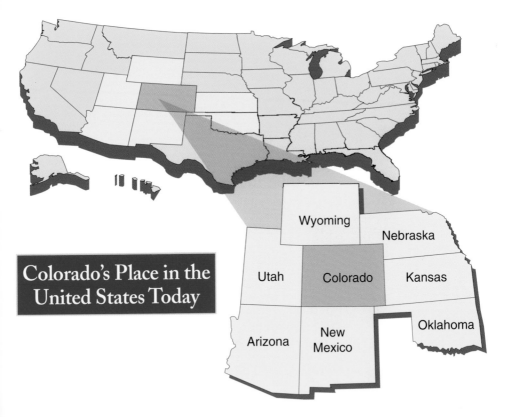

Colorado's Place in the United States Today

By the time the Basket Makers made their home in Colorado nearly five thousand years ago, the bones of extinct dinosaurs had long turned into fossils.

sorts of things, from holding possessions and preparing meals to sifting seeds and transporting water.

As time passed, the Basket Maker population grew and gained new knowledge. They came to depend on farming for much of their food. Bean crops were added, and turkeys were caught and raised on their farms for easy meals. As their society changed, basket weaving became less of a priority. The focus shifted to making pottery that could be used to hold foods and to aid in cooking over fires.

The Cliff Dwellers

One group of pottery makers became known as the Anasazi, or the "ancient ones." They lived in southwestern Colorado and the upper Rio Grande Valley in Texas, as well as areas in northeastern Arizona, northwestern New Mexico, and southeastern Utah.

The Anasazi depended greatly on agriculture. They grew corn, squash, and beans and built dams to collect water in **reservoirs**. The water was used to irrigate the crops, which grew well.

The Anasazi are remembered today for their villages called **pueblos**, which were located on the steep sides of mountains. Many of the pueblo buildings had hundreds of rooms and included grain storehouses and ceremonial chambers. The Anasazi cut down trees and used them to make roofs for most of the buildings. One building that still stands today in Colorado's

The Anasazi carved pictures of animals and other figures like these in and around their cliff dwellings.

Mesa Verde National Park is Cliff Palace. Cliff Palace was built under the overhang of a huge, open cave, and experts believe it dates all the way back to 1175. This amazing building contains 217 rooms and twenty-three kivas.

The Anasazi thrived from A.D. 900 to 1130. Crops grew well, despite an occasional drought, and food was plentiful. However, between 1150 and 1450, the Anasazi mysteriously abandoned their villages. Some moved to northeastern Arizona and western New Mexico. Scientists do not know what happened to the Anasazi. Some believe that a long-running drought forced them to find a new home. Others suspect that a religious crisis forced them to leave.

Giant kivas, like the one pictured here, provided a place for the Anasazi to store their grain. The Anasazi enjoyed plentiful crops for hundreds of years.

What is known is that the Anasazi had nearly disappeared by A.D. 1300. They left the plains and mountains of Colorado to small bands of **nomadic** hunters. Within about four hundred years, however, larger bands had moved into the region. These included the Ute, Kiowa, Comanche, Pawnee, Cheyenne, and Arapaho.

People from the "Land of the Sun"

The largest of these nomadic groups was the Ute. Their name means "land of the sun" or "people who dwell in the tops of mountains" because they originally settled in the mountains and highlands of the Rocky Mountains. Until 1868 over two-thirds of Colorado was home to the Ute. Those who lived in western and southern parts of Colorado lived in brush **wickiups**, pole-framed shelters that were usually covered with matting made from bark. Those who lived in the eastern section used animal-hide tepees. Usually the job of the women in the tribe was to build the shelters while the men hunted.

The Ute traditionally lived as nomads, moving with the seasons. They hunted with bows and arrows made of cedar wood and sheep horns and fashioned knives from flint. Hunters found deer, buffalo, elk, rabbits, and other small mammals on the mountain slopes and caught waterfowl in the many streams. Much of the meat was dried for the winter months when game was much harder to find. Furs were used for blankets and clothing.

Plants also made up an important part of their diet. Ute women gathered seed grasses, berries, roots, fruits, and greens. These were added to stews or dried for later use. As a tribe, the Ute would gather in the forests to collect the ripe nuts found in the pinecones of the piñon pine trees. These nuts were a main part of their overall diet. Men, women, and children spent days hitting the cones out of the trees with long sticks. They

Because the Anasazi lived along mountainsides and high cliffs, they built ladders like those pictured in this illustration to get from one part of a pueblo to another.

The Cliff Palace (pictured) is the most famous of the Anasazi buildings. The Anasazi lived and worked in the many rooms and kivas that make up the palace.

had to work hard and fast to get to the nuts before the animals did.

Once the Ute obtained horses and livestock from the Pueblo Indians of northern New Mexico in the early 1540s, life changed dramatically. Now they were able to raise animals themselves, raid or trade with other tribes, and protect themselves from their enemies. In some areas, the Ute became well known for being fierce warriors.

The Arapaho

Another hostile tribe in the area was the Arapaho. They lived on the plains from the Arkansas to the Platte Rivers in south central Nebraska. They were a nomadic tribe and had come to Colorado from the Red River in Canada. They fought with many other tribes in the area, including the Ute, whom they sometimes called their bravest enemies.

The Arapaho lifestyle was similar to that of the Ute. They lived in buffalo-skin tepees and spent much of their time hunting. Men within the Arapaho tribe often wore hip-leggings commonly made from deerskin, plus a breechcloth, robe, and moccasins. The women also wore moccasins with their dresses. Porcupine quills, paint, and beads were added for color and style.

Animal skins were an important part of Arapaho life. Buffalo skin was used to cover teepees, while deer skin was used for clothing and moccasins.

Unlike the Ute, though, the Arapaho used a special flat pipe for many of their religious ceremonies. The pipe had a stem almost two feet long, and the end of it was placed inside a bowl. It was kept hidden from the rest of the tribe until a special occasion came along. When it became necessary to pray for health or for an abundant food supply, for example, the men would bring it out and smoke it.

Even this special pipe, however, could not predict or help with the changes that were about to occur for most of Colorado's Indian tribes. Their lifestyles, from how they hunted to whom they battled, were about to undergo huge changes. In the mid-1500s, newcomers were going to discover the land—and they wanted it, too.

Chapter Two

Discovering the Land

The first outsiders to reach Colorado came in search of gold. Francisco Vásquez de Coronado, governor of a province in Mexico, is thought to have passed through a part of Colorado in 1540. He was on a mission to find the legendary Seven Golden Cities of Cibola somewhere in the southwestern United States. The tales of these fabled cities spoke of endless amounts of gold and fortune.

Coronado set off on his expedition from Mexico with one thousand Tlaxcalan Indians and three hundred Spanish soldiers. Over the next two years, the men searched for the cities throughout California, Colorado, and Arizona. They never found them. Instead, they found simple villages and Indians who knew nothing of the reputed treasures.

Coronado was determined to find the prized cities even after many of the others had given up. At one point, he sent his lieutenant, Garcia Lopez de Cardenas, to look further. That search did not turn up any gold but did lead to a remarkable find—the first European glimpse of the Grand Canyon.

Finally, in 1542, Coronado and the last of his men returned to Mexico in shame and disappointment. While the Spaniard had not found the treasure he had sought, he was one of the first Europeans to explore the North American Southwest. His descriptions of the Grand Canyon, of roaming buffalo, and of Indian village life fascinated people back home. In his report to the king in 1540, Coronado described a portion of the village lifestyle he found. "The food which they eat in this country is corn," he wrote, "of which they have

a great abundance and beans and venison which they probably eat (although they say they do not) because we found many skins of deer and hares and rabbits. They make the best corn cakes I have ever seen anywhere, and this is what everybody ordinarily eats."[1]

The following year, Coronado described the land:

> After nine day's march I reached some plains, so vast that I did not find their limit anywhere that I went, although I traveled over them for more than 300 leagues. And I found such a quantity of cows in these of the kind I wrote Your Majesty about, which they have in this country, that it is impossible to number them, for while I was journeying through these plains, until I

Francisco Vásquez de Coronado and his men trek through the Colorado plains. Coronado wrote detailed descriptions of the American Southwest.

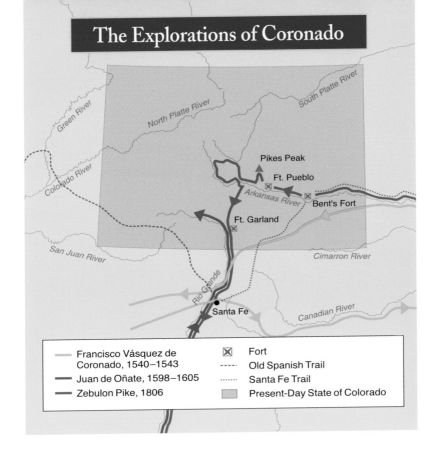

The Explorations of Coronado

Pikes Peak

Ft. Pueblo

Bent's Fort

Ft. Garland

Santa Fe

Green River
North Platte River
South Platte River
Colorado River
Arkansas River
San Juan River
Cimarron River
Rio Grande
Canadian River

— Francisco Vásquez de Coronado, 1540–1543	⊠	Fort
	----	Old Spanish Trail
— Juan de Oñate, 1598–1605	······	Santa Fe Trail
— Zebulon Pike, 1806	▨	Present-Day State of Colorado

returned to where I first found them, there was not a day that I lost sight of them.[2]

Continuing Explorations

In 1706 an expedition from New Mexico ventured out to the Arkansas River Valley, which runs throughout most of Colorado. Expedition leader Juan de Ulibarri claimed the region for Spain, naming it San Luis. It did not concern him that Robert La Salle had claimed the land for France back in 1682. Without set boundaries, control of Colorado passed back and forth between France and Spain for years.

Although the Spaniards of Mexico now had a new province to live in, they did not immediately settle there. Many were frightened by stories of Indian attacks. The Comanche, who lived mostly in the southern part of Colorado, tried to scare off the few Spaniards who passed through or settled there.

Despite the constant threat of Indian attack, exploration in this region of the country continued. In 1776 two new explorers entered Colorado territory. Francisco Antanasio Dominguez and Silvestre Velez de Escalante were Spanish priests searching for a northern route to Monterey, California. They wanted to establish missions throughout the area to help further the spread of Christianity.

The two priests and a dozen other men set off in late summer from Santa Fe, New Mexico. Their journey took them across the Great Basin Desert in western Colorado. In his journal Escalante wrote detailed descriptions of the land he saw, including an ancient Anasazi site. It is the first written account of a prehistoric site in Colorado. Heading north through western Colorado, the group got lost. They ran out of food and water and were eventually rescued by a band of Ute Indians. With two Ute guides, the expedition turned west and traveled into Utah, Arizona, and New Mexico. The return trip was no easier, and the group again encountered freezing rain, snow, and blizzard conditions, as well as a lack of provisions.

The priests never even came close to reaching California. However, the maps Escalante and Dominguez drew and the diaries they kept of their trip helped others know what was actually out there. It also helped to set up the Old Spanish Trail, a trade route running from Los Angeles, California, to Santa Fe, New Mexico, and passing through southwestern Colorado. Between 1830 and 1848, this trail saw Mexican and American traders taking woolen goods to the West and returning to the East with mules and horses.

Scouting It Out

The desire for increasing trade fueled other expeditions into Colorado. In 1806 General James Wilkinson, the commanding general of the U.S. Army, ordered military man Zebulon Montgomery Pike to explore

Zebulon Montgomery Pike explored the Great Plains and Rocky Mountains. His mission was to find possible trade routes and to buy land from the Indians.

Pikes Peak, named after Zebulon Pike, is the Rocky Mountains' highest peak.

the Great Plains and Rocky Mountains. Pike's job was to find the source of the Arkansas and Red Rivers so that the United States could establish trade routes. He was also instructed to purchase land from the Indians in the area.

Pike and twenty-two other men left Missouri in late summer of 1805. They did not succeed in finding the source of the Arkansas and Red Rivers. Pike did, however, send back descriptions of the land and climate of the region. In his reports, Pike described the Great Plains as **uninhabitable** and wrote that it was much like a huge desert. People who had been thinking about moving west now pictured sand dunes, blistering heat, and cactus and changed their minds. It would be a couple of decades before this mistake was corrected and people would once again look to Colorado as a promising new area to live.

Chapter Three

Mountain Men and War

By the sixteenth century, Spain had taken control of much of Colorado. Yet Spain did not actually establish any settlements there. As the land changed hands between the French and the Spanish, explorers came and went. It was not until the arrival of a new kind of explorer, the mountain man, that the land began to fill up with people ready to settle down.

The mountain men lived solitary lives, preferring to spend their time alone out in the world of nature rather than with people. Most had shoulder-length hair, long, tangled beards, and tanned skin. They wore buckskin clothes and carried pistols, knives, and traps for hunting and protection. They rarely had family, homes, money, or possessions. Instead, they slept outside, eating and living off the land and the buffalo, elk, and other game they caught. They moved from place to place with the seasons. While some traveled in groups of forty to sixty, breaking off into pairs to hunt, the majority forged out on their own.

The challenges of this kind of life were many. Mountain men endured freezing temperatures, Indian attacks, hungry grizzly bears, scarce food, and no medical care if they got sick or injured.

Mountain men earned their living trapping beavers. They traveled hundreds and sometimes thousands of miles in search of these animals. While they trapped, skinned, and traded other animals with the Indians, it was the beaver pelts that brought the most money.

A mountain man stops to let his horses drink. Mountain men earned a living by trapping beavers to sell to hat makers.

Beaver skin hats were all the rage back east in the 1820s and 1830s. Hatters were buying 100,000 pelts each year just to keep up with demand. Trappers could get between $6 and $9 for each pelt—a fortune in the early nineteenth century. As these men hunted, they also developed a wealth of knowledge about the territory through which they traveled. By 1840 when the beaver hat craze had died down, these men were forced to find other ways to make a living. Many of them ended up as wagon train guides, military scouts, and buffalo hunters. They used their knowledge of the area to help others find routes through the Colorado wilderness.

One such mountain man was James Beckwourth, an African American. He discovered a route to California through the Sierra Nevada mountains, which lie between California and Nevada. As a mountain man, he lived with the Crow Indians. Later he became a guide and scout, and in 1842 he helped form the original trading post that would be the start of the city of Pueblo, Colorado.

The routes that the mountain men established made settlement of Colorado possible. But little happened until the United States took control of eastern Colorado in 1803.

Part of the United States

In the 1803 Louisiana Purchase, the United States bought 800,000 square miles of land from France. This land purchase reached from the Gulf of Mexico to the upper region of Montana and from the Missis-

British North America
Massachusetts
Vermont
New Hampshire

Oregon Country

New York

Rhode Island
Connecticut
New Jersey
Pennsylvania
Delaware
Maryland

Present-day Colorado

Louisiana Purchase 1803

Indiana Territory

Ohio

Virginia

Kentucky

Tennessee

North Carolina

South Carolina

Mississippi Territory

Georgia

New Spain

Spanish Florida

Colorado Lands during the Louisiana Purchase

sippi River to Montana and Idaho. It doubled the size of the United States for $15 million, or about three cents per acre.

President Thomas Jefferson immediately commissioned explorers Meriwether Lewis and William Clark to travel to the lands in the West to discover what was there. Their detailed reports, drawings, and artifacts excited the imagination of many people. The public began to look to the West as a possible place to live rather than as a frightening wilderness.

Now that the eastern half of Colorado was under the control of the United States, families felt safer in moving there. In 1833 Colorado's first permanent non-Indian settlement was finally finished. Called Bent's Fort, it was located on the Santa Fe Trail near the Arkansas River in what is now called East La Junta,

Bent's Fort was established as Colorado's first permanent non-Indian settlement. Hunters and Indians traded goods there, and travelers used it as a hotel.

Colorado. It was built by brothers William and Charles Bent and their partner, Ceran St. Vrain, some of the area's first white settlers. The place served not only as a trading post for hunters and Indians to trade furs and pelts, but also as a hotel for people passing through from one area to another.

Bent's Fort did not have a very long life. During the war of 1846, U.S. soldiers looking for food and supplies ransacked it. Although they promised the Bents that the government would pay them back for all of it, the money did not come as promised, and William Bent became angry. Rather than see the rest of his fort go to the government, he put kegs of gunpowder all around the place and blew up almost the entire site.

Mexico and America Go to War

By the early 1840s the eastern part of Colorado had a smattering of settlers. The western portion still belonged to Mexico, along with much of the rest of the West. During this time the United States embarked on a drive to expand across the continent all the way to the Pacific Ocean. This effort was known as manifest destiny. Manifest destiny described Americans' belief that they had a God-given right to own these western lands, even if someone was already living there.

The United States finally won control of the western half of Colorado in 1848, following war with Mexico. On February 2, 1848, the Treaty of Guadalupe Hidalgo was signed, ending the war. The United States

Future president Zachary Taylor confers with officers during the Mexican–American War. After the war ended in 1848, the United States owned all of Colorado.

paid Mexico $15 million for the territories of western Colorado, California, Nevada, Arizona, New Mexico, Wyoming, and Utah.

Now all of Colorado belonged to the United States, but it was proving even harder to attract new-comers to the western half than it was to the eastern half. It was hard to get there, and no one knew what they would find if they made the trip. However, the appeal of Colorado did grow, and the key to its growth was the lure, fascination, and promise of G-O-L-D.

Chapter Four

Gold and Statehood

Gold fever had struck Colorado! In 1858 William Green Russell found the first gold in Cherry Creek, a tributary of the South Platte River, near today's Denver suburbs. It was a small piece, only worth several hundred dollars, but it was enough to spark a huge interest. Word that gold had been found in Colorado spread quickly east. People there were in the midst of an economic depression and were worried by the first rumors of a coming civil war. Moving offered a way to avoid both. More than 100,000 people headed west within the next two years.

Almost half of those who went in search of gold returned home empty-handed. The rest remained, boosting the population of Colorado and becoming the starting point for most of its cities. Denver got its start this way, as did other cities. The cities of Golden, Boulder, Central City, and Colorado City were formed, for example, when George Jackson and John Gregory struck it rich just west of Denver. In 1860 prospector Abe Lee found gold nuggets at the bottom of California Gulch west of Denver. From this find, Oro City was started.

Within five years of forming, most of these cities had churches, schools, and businesses. The people who made the most were those who opened up general stores to provide food, equipment, and clothing to the miners or built hotels to house them. Their goods were often paid for in pinches of gold dust, or what could be held between the thumb and index finger of the average man. Each pinch was worth about a quarter, and because everything had to be shipped in, prices were high. A bag of potatoes often went as high as $15, and eggs were one dollar each.

A traveler making the rough journey to Colorado stops to rest near his wagon. In just two years, more than 100,000 people headed west in search of gold.

Prospectors pan for gold in a Colorado stream. The thousands of gold seekers that flocked to Colorado formed the basis for the population of cities like Denver and Boulder.

Among those who came to Colorado during this time period was Catherine Murat, a German immigrant who sewed and flew the first Colorado flag. In 1859 Elizabeth and William Byers moved to Denver from Ohio and started the first newspaper, the *Rocky Mountain News*, which is still being published today.

A Territory and a War

By 1860 Colorado had reached a population of 34,277. The following year, Congress declared it an official territory, and there was already talk of statehood in the future. William Gilpin was made governor, and the area continued to expand the thrive. However, troubled times lay ahead.

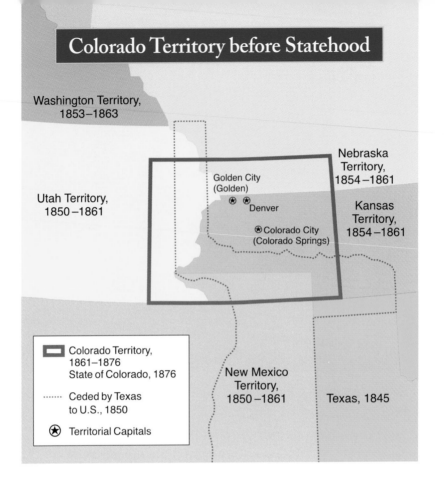

Colorado Territory before Statehood

Washington Territory, 1853–1863

Nebraska Territory, 1854–1861

Utah Territory, 1850–1861

Kansas Territory, 1854–1861

Golden City (Golden)

⊛ ⊛ Denver

⊛ Colorado City (Colorado Springs)

Colorado Territory, 1861–1876
State of Colorado, 1876

Ceded by Texas to U.S., 1850

⊛ Territorial Capitals

New Mexico Territory, 1850–1861

Texas, 1845

In 1862 the Civil War began. Colorado's first cavalry was put together soon after, and they fought on the Union side, helping to keep the Confederate army from reaching California. At the same time, Colorado was also battling another war—the ongoing battle for land between the Native Americans and the settlers.

Battle of Sandy Creek

In the early part of the 1860s Cheyenne and Arapaho Indians were raiding settlers all over Colorado after being pushed off their land too many times. They were running out of places to hunt and to find food to eat. Under the Fort Laramie Treaty of 1851, they had been given a reservation in southeastern Colorado, but the soil was bad, game was scarce, and diseases were killing many of their people. In desperation, Cheyenne chief Black Kettle and over seven hundred of his people came to Fort Lyon to talk with the governor about a compromise. They were turned away and told to wait nearby. They set up camp forty miles away at Sandy Creek, believing that they were in safe territory under the protection of the U.S. government, which expressly stated that the military was to take no action against these tribes.

However, Colonel John Chivington, a man who thought the only way to deal with Indians was to kill

Cheyenne Indian warriors clash with U.S. soldiers in this painting of the Battle of Sandy Creek.

them, did not see things that way. He hoped to secure a victory against these Indians that would promote him to brigadier general. To do this, he recruited a cavalry of 750 volunteers and formed them into the Third Colorado Regiment. On November 29, 1864, in the dark of night, he and his men attacked the Indians. They ignored both the American flag and the white flag flying over the camp. Over two hundred Indians were killed, most of them women and children. Chivington was later found guilty of unworthy conduct.

Life for Colorado's Native American people grew steadily worse as more settlers arrived. Ranchers and farmers continued to push the tribes off their land. People kept coming to Colorado, determined to find gold or at least a new beginning. By 1881, almost all Native American tribes had been pushed out of Colorado. Many of them moved to reservations in other states.

After the Battles

After the Civil War ended, Colorado once again turned its attention to becoming a state. The first real effort in 1864 failed. The Coloradoans rejected a proposed constitution, 5,006 to 4,219. Many believed that Colorado could not yet afford self-governance. Mines were not producing as hoped. Word had once again spread about gold—but this time it was to warn people that it was not easy to find. Fearing a financial disaster, the people voted against the constitution.

Although towns were dying across the region, some settlers were determined to make their home a state.

They began to market the West. Using a new invention called a camera, they took pictures of the beautiful country and sent them back east. They wrote stories and did everything they could to interest people in moving to Colorado.

Getting people's attention about Colorado was the first step. The complication came in how to get them there. The solution arrived with the help of a railroad man named William Jackson Palmer. He knew that other rail lines were bypassing Colorado because of the Rocky Mountains, so he built the Denver and Rio Grande Railroad, a north-south line that opened the mountains to travelers. Palmer hoped new cities would

This idealized painting depicts the admission of Colorado into the Union. In 1876 Colorado became the thirty-eighth state.

grow along his rail line. This is exactly what happened. The cities of Pueblo, Trinidad, and Colorado Springs formed as people began to use the new railroad.

In 1865 a new constitution was put to a vote. This time it passed, but statehood did not immediately follow. Two things conspired to slow it down. First Abraham Lincoln had been assassinated, and Andrew Johnson, a Democrat, had replaced him. Johnson was not looking to add any Republican states to the Union at this point, and Colorado tended to vote Republican. In addition, the spreading news of the massacre at Sandy Creek hurt Colorado's image. Supporters began to back away. President Johnson vetoed the constitution, and from 1869 to 1873, attempts to bring the state into the Union failed again and again.

A break finally came in 1875. Colorado had grown quite a bit and now had more than 135,000 people, the minimum number needed to be considered for statehood. The new constitution passed with 19,483 votes to 15,830.

On August 1, 1876, Colorado was made the thirty-eighth state. Since its statehood occurred almost at the same time that the United States celebrated one hundred years of independence, Colorado is often called the Centennial State. With its rich history of Native Americans, explorers, and settlers, it is little surprise that the state has always attracted those with adventure in their hearts.

Notes

Chapter Two: Discovering the Land

1. Quoted in "The West," www.pbs.org.
2. Quoted in "The West," www.pbs.org.

Facts About Colorado

State capital: Denver

State song: "Where the Columbines Grow"

State motto: *Nil sine numine* (Nothing without Providence)

State nicknames: Centennial State, Mother of Rivers

State tree: blue spruce

State animal: bighorn sheep

State fish: greenback cutthroat trout

State bird: lark bunting

State flower: Rocky Mountain columbine

State insect: Colorado hairstreak butterfly

State fossil: stegosaurus

State Gemstone: aquamarine

Wildlife: bighorn sheep, mountain goats, mountain lions, deer, elk, black bears, beavers, foxes, coyotes, prairie dogs, eagles, marmots, Colorado chipmunks, bobcats, pronghorn antelopes, lark buntings, falcons, hawks, hummingbirds, rattlesnakes, black widow spiders, trout, perch, catfish, bass

Farm products: beef, cattle, horses, milk, lettuce, cherries, pears, plums, potatoes, dry beans, barley, apples, peaches, wheat, sugar beets, hay, corn, cucumbers, tomatoes, watermelon

Mining products: oil, natural gas, coal, gold, silver, and uranium

Manufactured products: brick

Business and trade: tourism, printing and publishing, food products

Famous people: Tim Allen (actor), Black Kettle (Native American leader), Malcolm Scott Carpenter (astronaut), Lon Chaney (actor), Clive Cussler (author), Jack Dempsey (boxer), John Denver (singer), Douglas Fairbanks (actor), Ruth Handler (toy maker), Willard Libby (chemist), Hattie McDaniel (actress), James Michener (author), Glenn Miller (band conductor), Patricia Schroeder (congresswoman)

Places to Visit in Colorado

Boulder: Buffalo Bill Museum and Grave, Leanin' Tree Museum of Western Art

Canyon City: Buckskin Joe Frontier Town and Railway

Colorado Springs: Cheyenne Mountain Zoo, Colorado Springs Fine Art Center, Pikes Peak Ghost Town, Santa's Workshop

Denver: Colorado History Museum, Denver Art Museum, Denver Botanical Gardens, Denver Museum of Nature and Science, Denver Zoo, Six Flags Elitch Gardens, Water World

Dinosaur: Dinosaur National Monument

Durango: Durango and Silverton Narrow Gauge Railway and Museum

Estes Park: Rocky Mountain National Park

Florissant: Florissant Fossil Beds National Monument

Fruita: Colorado National Monument, Colorado River State Park

Georgetown: Georgetown Loop Railway

Golden: Golden Gate Canyon State Park

Manitou Springs: Cave of the Winds, Manitou Cliff Dwellings, Pikes Peak Cog Railway

Mesa Verde: Mesa Verde National Park, Yucca House National Monument

Mosca: Colorado Gators Farm, Great Sand Dunes National Monument and Preserve

Nathrop: St. Elmo Ghost Town

Pueblo: Bent's Old Fort National Historic Site, Pueblo History Museum

Silverton: Durango and Silverton Narrow Gauge Railway, Old Hundred Gold Mine

Glossary

atelatl: An ancient device that helped hunters throw a spear with great power.

kiva: Underground pit for storing grain.

mesa: Flat-topped mountain.

nomadic: People who wandered and did not settle in one place for long.

pueblo: Small Indian village.

reservoir: A chamber for storing a fluid like rainwater.

uninhabitable: Not capable of being lived in.

wickiup: A frame hut covered with matting made from bark or brush.

For Further Exploration

Eleanor Ayer, *The Anasazi*. New York: Walker, 1993.

Jean Blashfield, *Colorado*. Chicago: Childrens Press, 1999.

Sylvester Ellis, *The Life of Kit Carson*. Fort Collins, CO: Lost Classics Book Company, 2001.

Alice Flanagan, *The Utes*. Chicago: Childrens Press, 1998.

Jan Gleiter and Kathleen Thompson, *Kit Carson*. Austin, TX: Raintree/Steck-Vaughn, 1996.

Timothy Larson, *Anasazi*. Austin, TX: Raintree/Steck-Vaughn, 2001.

Kay Matthews, *An Anasazi Welcome*. Santa Fe, NM: Red Crane Books, 1992.

Emily McAuliffe, *Colorado Facts and Symbols*. Mankato, MN: Bridgestone Books, 1998.

Jan Pettit, *Utes: The Mountain People*. Boulder, CO: Johnson Books, 1990.

Charles W. Sundling, *Mountain Men of the Frontier*. Edina, MN: Abdo and Daughters, 2000.

Jim Whiting, *Francisco Vasquez de Coronado*. Bear, DE: Mitchell Lane, 2002.

Barbara Witteman, *Zebulon Pike: Soldier and Explorer*. Mankato, MN: Bridgestone Books, 2002.

Index

Picture Credits

About the Author

Tamra B. Orr is a full-time writer and author living in Portland, Oregon. She graduated from Ball State University in 1982 and is the author of almost a dozen nonfiction books for children and families, including *The Parent's Guide to Homeschooling*. She homeschools her four children, ages eighteen to six, who, she says, teach her more every single day. In her six spare minutes a day, she loves to read, sit in the sunshine, and admire the Northwest mountains.